OXFORD
UNIVERSITY PRESS

Great Clarendon Street, Oxford, OX2 6DP, United Kingdom

Oxford University Press is a department of the University of Oxford. It furthers the University's objective of excellence in research, scholarship, and education by publishing worldwide. Oxford is a registered trade mark of Oxford University Press in the UK and in certain other countries

Text © Oxford University Press 2023

The moral rights of the author have been asserted

First Edition published in 2023

All rights reserved. No part of this publication may be reproduced, stored in a retrieval system, or transmitted, in any form or by any means, without the prior permission in writing of Oxford University Press, or as expressly permitted by law, by licence or under terms agreed with the appropriate reprographics rights organization. Enquiries concerning reproduction outside the scope of the above should be sent to the Rights Department, Oxford University Press,
at the address above.

You must not circulate this work in any other form and you must impose this same condition on any acquirer

British Library Cataloguing in Publication Data

Data available

ISBN: 978-1-382-04345-8

10 9 8 7 6 5 4 3 2

The manufacturing process conforms to the environmental regulations of the country of origin.

Printed in China by Golden Cup

Acknowledgements

Rainforest Rescue and Look into a Rainforest written by Liz Miles.

Artwork by Aleksandar Zolotić, Kate McKelland, Laszlo Veres and Dan Lewis.

The publisher and author would like to thank the following for permission to use photographs and other copyright material:

Photos: back cover: Thorsten Spoerlein / Shutterstock; p5(bkg): Free Ukraine and Belarus / Shutterstock; p12-13(bkg): ImagePost / Shutterstock; p45: worldclassphoto / Shutterstock; p48(bkg): Galen Rowell / Corbis Documentary / Getty Images; p48(l): Tarcisio Schnaider / Shutterstock; p48(r): PARALAXIS / Shutterstock; p49: Dr Morley Read / Shutterstock; p50(t): PhotocechCZ / Shutterstock; p50(b): E Michael James / iStock / Getty Images; p51: Gabrielle Therin-Weise / Getty Images; p52-53: earlytwenties / Shutterstock; p53(inset): tc397 / iStock / Getty Images; p54: Daniel Lamborn / Shutterstock; p55: Thomas Janisch / Moment / Getty Images; p56(bkg): Free Ukraine and Belarus / Shutterstock; p56: culbertson / iStock / Getty Images; p57: Thorsten Spoerlein / Shutterstock; p58-59: Octavio Campos Salles / Alamy Stock Photo; p59(inset): Lucas Leuzinger / Shutterstock; p60(t): Dirk Ercken / Shutterstock; p60(b): Pedro Turrini Neto / Shutterstock; p61: Michael Siluk / Shutterstock; p62(bkg): Free Ukraine and Belarus / Shutterstock; p62: EMPPhotography / iStock / Getty Images; p63: Atosan / Shutterstock; p66: Reto Buehler / Shutterstock; p67(t): Minden Pictures / Alamy Stock Photo; p67(b): Grigorii Pisotsckii / Shutterstock; p68: PARALAXIS / Shutterstock; p68(inset): ERNESTO BENAVIDES / AFP via Getty Images.

Every effort has been made to contact copyright holders of material reproduced in this book. Any omissions will be rectified in subsequent printings if notice is given to the publisher.

In this book ...

Rainforest Rescue 11

Look Into a Rainforest 43

Have a go!

ay as in play

ou as in count

ie as in magpie

ea as in seat

oy as in toy

ir as in skirt

ue as in glue

aw as in lawn

oh

their

people

Mrs

Mr

Read this book if ...

you love

ANIMAL RESCUES

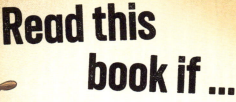

and

DEEP, DARK FORESTS!

In this book, Shackleton looks for a lost animal.

What was the last thing you lost?
How did you feel?

RAINFOREST ADVENTURE

Written by Liz Miles
Illustrated by Aleksandar Zolotić

Shackleton
(say: Shack-ul-tun)

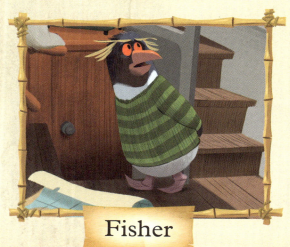

Fisher

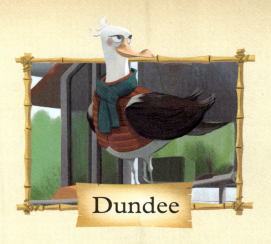

Dundee

Tash the tamarin

Shackleton and his pals, Fisher and Dundee, like to travel. They often end up helping someone in need.

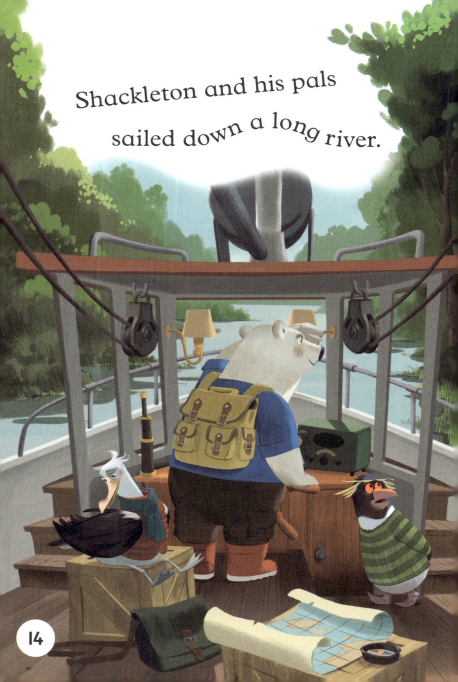
Shackleton and his pals sailed down a long river.

"We have reached the
Amazon rainforest!"
said Shackleton.

"Oh! What was that?" squeaked Fisher.

"A **beast** that eats people and birds!" said Dundee.

"It was just me!" squawked a blue macaw. "Tash the tamarin is **missing!**"

"Yes! We will help you," Shackleton said.

Shackleton and Fisher attached the ship to a tree.

A pair of tamarins explained what happened.

"Tash **disappeared** at midday!" wept Mr Beard.

"He is **lost**!" said Mrs Twirl.

"We will rescue Tash!"
boomed Shackleton.

"Fisher will check the river," said Shackleton.

"Tash! Are you there?"
Fisher shouted.

He swam along
until he felt a **NIP!**

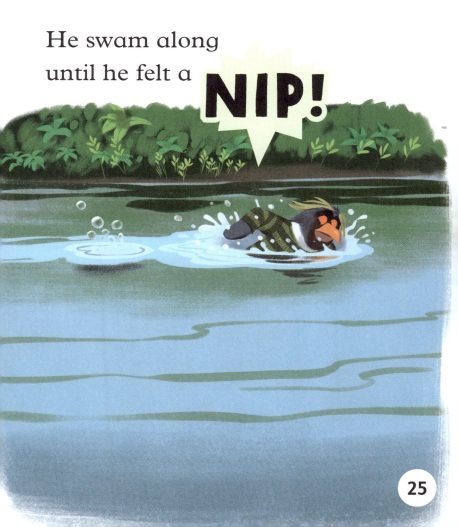

Fisher crawled up the bank.

"I will **creep** into the forest," said Shackleton. "I can sniff out Tash!"

Shackleton **crept** along the path. He sniffed the ground with his snout.

Then a trail of ants found him.
Shackleton ran back to the ship!

"I will look for Tash," sighed Dundee.

Dundee swirled and swooped, scanning the treetops.

Then there was a **sharp** sound.

Dundee looked around.

"It is just me again,"
screeched the blue macaw.

Then Dundee spotted Tash.

"Tash is trapped," Dundee said.

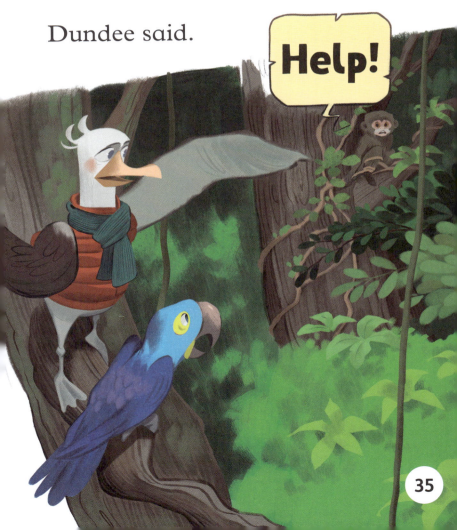

Tash was *tangled* in a creeper.

"I am Dundee. We will rescue you," Dundee said.

Dundee and the macaw **snapped** off the creeper.

"Thank you!" said Tash.

SNAP!

"You found Tash!" boomed Shackleton. He was proud of Dundee.

"Let's set sail!" said Fisher.

"The ship is stuck in the **mud**," said Shackleton.

"We will help you!" squawked the macaw.

A flock of macaws *tugged* them free. The tamarins chirped as they sailed away.

Look back

1. What had happened to Tash?

2. How do you think Dundee felt when she found Tash?

3. Do you think Shackleton and his pals enjoyed visiting the rainforest?

In this book, we will look into the Amazon rainforest.

What sorts of animals might you see in a rainforest?

LOOK INTO A RAINFOREST

Written by Liz Miles
Illustrated by Laszlo Veres
and Dan Lewis

Contents

Rainforests 44

In the treetops 48

Under the trees 52

On the ground 58

In the river 64

Rescue the forest! 68

Look it up and Index .. 69

Rainforests

Rainforests are hot and wet.
They are full of trees.

South America

- rainforests
- Amazon rainforest

The Amazon rainforest is in South America.

River Amazon

The Amazon rainforest has layers.

You can see different things growing in each layer.

In the treetops

High in the forest there is lots of light.

seed pods

nuts

Nuts grow on some trees. They grow in seed pods.

FOREST FACT

Trees can grow as high as 30 stacked buses.

Birds perch to eat nuts.

Bats enjoy **fluttering** around at night.

Eagles

This eagle **GRABS** animals to eat.

Then it swoops down to the ground.

sharp beak

strong claws

51

Under the trees

It is damp under the trees. Animals stay hidden in the shadows.

FOREST FACT
This plant **TRAPS** insects to eat.

A hummingbird sips **nectar** from flowers.

long beak

Anacondas **GRAB** birds and lizards.

FOREST FACT

Anacondas can be as long as a bus!

This insect **mimics** a leaf! It likes to stay hidden in the trees.

Stay away!

Some Amazon frogs are **toxic**. Their goo can kill you.

On the ground

The ground level is the darkest layer. There are mounds of rotting plants.

A **BIG** animal like this might **creep** about!

This cat has big paws.

Some paths can be crowded.

leaf-cutter ants

FOREST FACT
The ants have sharp jaws!

An anteater might **pursue** the ants.

Tree roots

BIG trees need **BIG** roots to support them.

Some roots grow out from the tree trunk.

In the river

Amazon River fact
There are at least 2400 different sorts of fish.

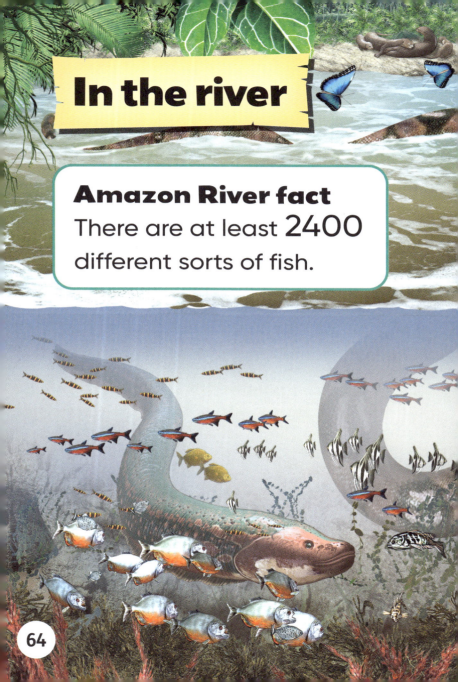

Anacondas swim around, looking for fish to eat.

Otters play in the river.

SPLASH

This fish mimics a leaf.

This fish has **sharp** teeth!

Rescue the forest!

Animals suffer if trees are cut down.

Growing trees is best!

Look it up

mimics: looks like

nectar: sweet liquid formed by plants

pursue: follow

toxic: harmful

Index

anacondas 55, 65

ants 60, 61, 62

birds 50, 51, 54

fish 64, 65, 67

trees 44, 48, 49, 63, 68

Ha! Ha!

What do you call a rainforest that is fast asleep?

The Pajamazon!